BETTY OLELA

Navigating The United States of America

America

A Guideline For New Immigrants

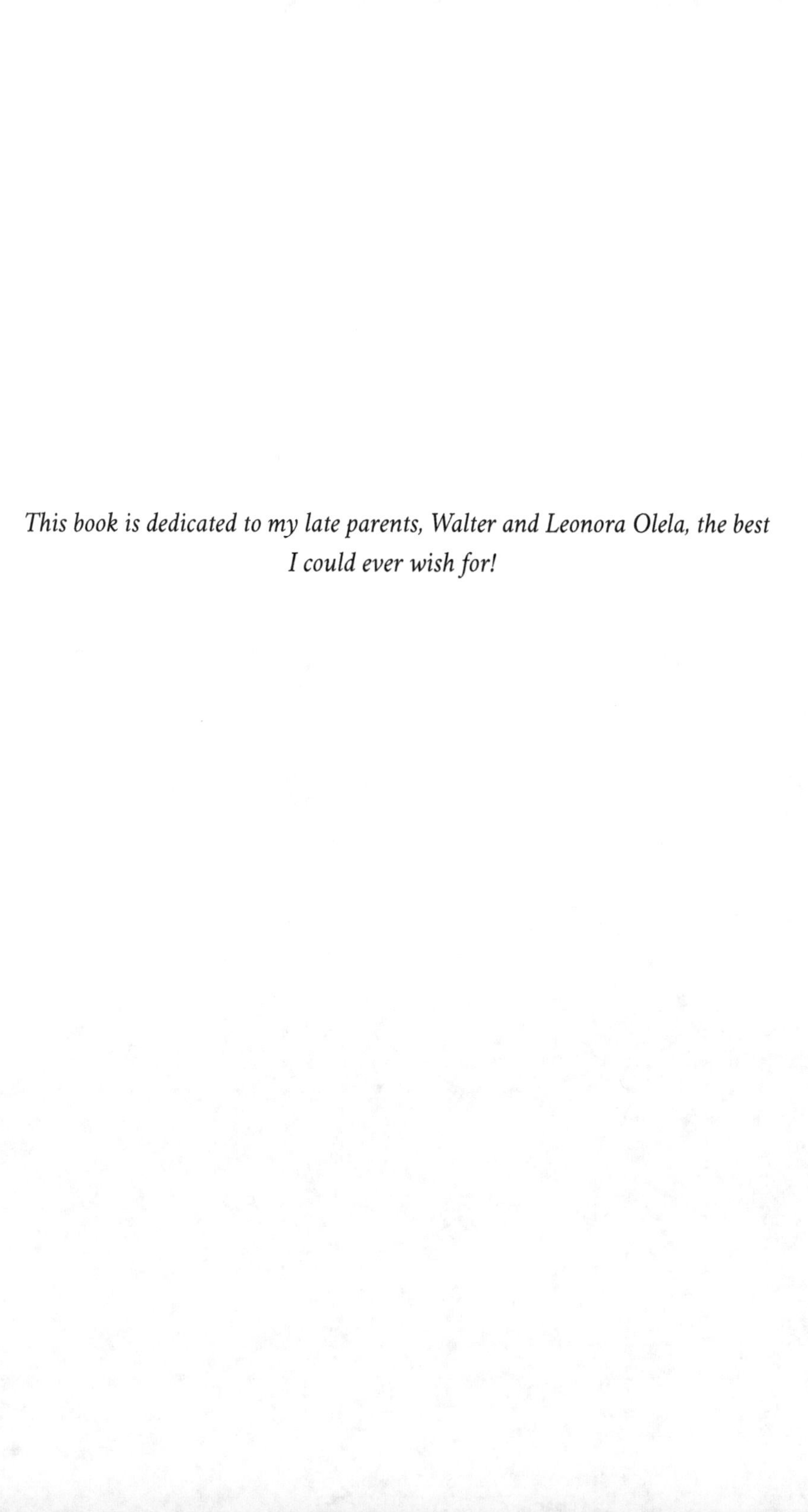

This book is dedicated to my late parents, Walter and Leonora Olela, the best I could ever wish for!

Contents

Acknowledgement

I am most grateful to my children, Michelle and Eric, for their encouragement and unwavering support. They migrated to the United States a few months before me but adapted to their new environment so fast they were able to hold my hands through the initial days of culture shock. Secondly, many thanks to my uncle, Maurice who was my host when I moved to the USA.

Special appreciation to my first employer, Mr. Pecorari who set the stage for my life in the United States. No amount of words can adequately capture our respect and gratitude to you and your family for all your kindness to us. More thanks to my publisher Roy; for his words of encouragement; guiding me through the process of having a book published; and turning my dream of becoming an author a reality by publishing my first book.

Finally, I want to thank everyone else who contributed in one way or another to this process. Every word of motivation counted; every act of kindness appreciated.

Introduction

Getting an immigrant visa to relocate to the United States can come with a symphony of emotions: exciting thrills mixed with apprehensive anxiety. The thought of starting a new life in a mighty, sophisticated, and diverse country like the United States can be overwhelming. There is so much to plan and so much to know. But all these are dimmed by the delightful pleasure of finally having the possibility to live the life of your dreams. The elation of living the American Dream.

Moving to a new place comes with its fair share of stress—sometimes more and sometimes less. There are a lot of logistical issues to consider, for example, knowing what part of the new country to choose as your new home, what personal effects to carry along with you, issues regarding money, work, and housing, and handling the imminent culture shock that comes with relocation.

I write this book from a position of personal experience, having relocated to the United States a few years ago, enriched by my background as a trained teacher and educator for many years. I graduated with a Bachelor of Education from Moi University (Kenya) and earned a Master's in education from Egerton University (Kenya).

My education and knowledge helped me not only to adjust quickly to my new home but also to be aware of the intricacies of this life and how emotional intelligence and sound decision-making can help one avoid unnecessary mistakes and hurdles in the process of settling down as a new immigrant.

Interestingly, I never quite planned to migrate to the United States. I came to visit my kids, who had relocated to the country the previous year. My son, who had a green card then, was almost turning twenty-one years old, so I decided to wait for him to petition for my permanent residency. That was a spontaneous decision. I intended to be in the United States for only three weeks and then return to my old life in Kenya, working two jobs and running a cybercafé business on the side.

My uncle hosted me for the first few weeks. I had come in the summer, and there were several social events and parties hosted by fellow immigrants that we attended, and I was able to meet and make friends with several women from my country. From these interactions, I learned about working as domestic help and living with the family you worked for. I also learned how to get these jobs on the internet.

Consequently, I put an advert on Craigslist offering my services as domestic help and got a job as a live-in housekeeper with a family in Pennsylvania. Living with this family formed the foundation of my new life in the United States. Because they were well-to-do, I learned the full circle of American life and culture through the four seasons: summer, fall, winter, and spring.

I learned about the various American holidays and their associated activities, like how important Thanksgiving is, the various dishes cooked at Thanksgiving, and how they are prepared. I learned to do elaborate Christmas decorations (which they did on a scale I had never seen before) and to use the many appliances and gadgets in American homes and everything else that came with an affluent lifestyle!

Most importantly, I learned about American culture, what was politically correct in polite conversations, and what was not. I learned about fashion and top designers like Gucci, Louis Vuitton, and all those wildly expensive designers. I learned to swim, ride a bike, cook various dishes, and mix a basic cocktail. I learned the basics of football and adopted the fanatical following of the Philadelphia Eagles. I must have taken a million photos while living in this home because everything was glamorous and exciting.

I worked in this home for two years, then moved to the city of Philadelphia, where I got an authentic taste of life as a new immigrant. Suddenly, I was on my own and had to navigate city life with no road map. It was the first time I was getting an apartment and all the related utilities that come with it. Even worse, I moved to Philadelphia in January (winter) of 2020, just before COVID hit!

I had moved to pursue a "better job" but lost the job three months later. And for a while, I could not get a job due to the quarantine. Life became a struggle. I had to learn fast. I knew my priority was to get a job—any job. And to pay the rent diligently, whatever the case.

Years later, having interacted with many new immigrants, I have learned that not everyone gets lucky to get a soft landing. Many people cannot find someone to host them the first few months they get into the country and have to live in motels. Others get very hostile or mean hosts who demean them or take advantage of their naivety and vulnerability. Some find themselves entirely alone and must fumble and stumble until they find their footing.

Such difficult beginnings are likely to chip away at one's foundation and affect the pace at which they integrate into their new home. Not having the correct information can be a painful and expensive experience. Many people had such bad experiences during the first few months/years of their stay in the United States that they abandoned the dream and returned to their home countries.

The Great Move

"My family and I came to America in an open boat with just the clothes on our backs" is a common saying amongst many immigrants to the United States. An entry into the United States of America presents one with endless opportunities to live the life of their dreams, aka the American Dream.

A life of glamour, opulence, and luxury. Wearing designer outfits and spending vacations on exotic islands. Driving flashy sports cars or big SUV vehicles you previously only saw in movies. A dream to earn six-figure incomes that would afford us a happily-ever-after life!

Leaving the familiarity of your home, friends, and social life is such a significant milestone that it would be good to adequately prepared for the move mentally, physically, and financially.

The most logical thing to do before making your move is to get a host who is already living in the US to take you through what to expect. The host could be a family member or a friend; an American, or a fellow immigrant.

Having a host will help you sort out the decision of what state to choose as your new home, as you will go to the state where they live. Your host would be the one to pick you up from the airport and help you overcome the initial culture shock many people experience when they reach the United States, as well as give you some sense of belonging.

He/she can help you acquire a phone number and, if possible, open a bank account as a matter of priority. A lot of transactions in the US are cashless; therefore, it is important to open a bank account and link that account to your phone so you can access services through the apps on your phone.

The host is likely be busy chasing their American Dream and may not have the time to drive you around or attend to your needs. Once you have a working phone and a bank account linked to it, you should learn to use the internet to get whatever you need.

For example, use the internet to find public transport near you; install ride-sharing apps like Uber or Lyft and use them to get around. Use the internet to search for and know whatever stores or services you may want and how far they are from you. You can literally run your whole life from your phone.

Make yourself useful while being hosted. Help around the house. Find out from your host what you can do to help. You could help mow the lawn, fold laundry, walk kids to the bus, or run errands like grocery shopping or going to the post office. Most people living in the United States work long hours or multiple jobs and are so overwhelmed that they would appreciate some help. Do not become a couch potato by just scrolling through the TV channels and eating all the snacks in the house.

It is easier to adapt to a new place when you learn the culture of the people. Americans have such a distinct way of doing their things that it would be vital for you to have some idea of American culture. For instance, American English is very distinct from British English; they say elevator, not lift; trunk, not boot; muffins, not queen cake. Also, Americans are big on courtesy words and phrases such as "please" and "thank you." Catch on to the trend.

Do not be bothered so much with your accent but more with speaking in a clear manner that other people can understand. Your accent forms part of your identity and authenticity, so there is no point in losing sleep over it. If you live in this country long enough and interact with Americans, you will eventually pick up the American accent, if you want to.

Learn a few things about your new environment. You can easily do this by browsing the internet. Learn the geography of your immediate neighborhood and know what is where. Know the public parks and libraries around you so you can spend time there. Learn the lifestyle of the people around you and know what is acceptable to say or do, and what is not. Americans are big on sports and are very passionate about the local sports teams. Get to know what sports are popular in your city/township and the names of the teams. This makes for polite conversation in social circles.

Two very vital American cultures that you must be sensitive to, so as not to offend anyone with your ignorance, are pets and sexual orientation. Pets are considered members of the family, and pet owners would expect you to treat and address their pets as you would a child or a member of the family. Please do not touch or pet anyone's dog (or cat) without their permission.

Accept and respect, without question, people's choices on issues of sex and sexual orientation. Just be warned that it can be very illustrative in this country. Keep your sentiments about the issue very private, just as you should keep silent about people's manner of dressing. You will see a lot. Religion is a touchy matter that is likely to provoke intense differences in opinions; you may also want to respect people's choices in this regard.

Food is abundant and affordable. The servings in restaurants are so large that people often ask for doggy bags to carry the remnants home. Go slow on processed meats and junk food, especially if your body is not used to them. The United States has a wide variety of farm produce, and you will find foods you are familiar with. This is particularly important to help you retain your body weight. Obesity is a thing in the United

States.

In most cities and/or townships, there are small corner stores that sell foods from various parts of the world so that you are likely to get your favorite food from your motherland if you want to. For example, there are stores that sell Indian food, we have West African stores that sell delicacies from that region. There are stores that sell Kenyan foods or Ethiopian stores, or Korean stores or Mexican stores and so on. These stores will be found in neighborhoods where there are many people from that region living.

Most of this information you can find on social media or through Google search. Some industrious immigrants have resorted to growing some of the unique herbs and vegetables from their motherland in their backyards, many times for own use but sometimes to sell. Amazon is also known to stock a wide variety of condiments and foodstuffs from various parts of the world.

Therefore, you can eat in this country, the very foods you ate in your homeland if you want to avoid eating junk. You will be surprised how eating familiar foods helps minimize homesickness.

The United States of America has about 50 states, most of which are vastly different from each other. The country is divided into the East Coast, West Coast, South, and Mid-West. The East Coast gets very cold, especially in the winter, as does the Mid-West. The West Coast is cold to the north and warm to the south. The South is warm throughout the year, with no winters, but it can get extremely hot in the summer. Whichever state you settle in, always know the day's weather before you leave the house because the weather can be unpredictable and severe.

Where possible, schedule your travel to the United States before the cold season/winter. This allows you room to deal with the other issues related to relocation before you can deal with the shock of just how cold it can get in the winter. It also allows your body to slowly adjust since the decrease in temperatures is gradual. No amount of information can adequately prepare you for the misery and challenges of the cold season, especially if it is the first season you get to experience. Winter is brutal and relentless; icy temperatures, shorter days, and longer nights, sometimes with terrible snowstorms, other times the sun may be shining brightly but temperatures are below freezing point.

It is important to dress appropriately for the winter weather. Even though houses and cars are all heated and you may never feel cold while indoors, always carry a winter coat (as well as gloves, a scarf, and a hat if possible) when leaving the house. The car can break down or there can be a situation that leads to you being outdoors longer than you planned. Even just 5 minutes outdoors during winter can be detrimental to your health if you do not dress appropriately. There is the danger of pneumonia, hypothermia or even frostbite.

Take note that winter outfits are pricier and plan accordingly. Ride share apps like Uber or Lyft are also more expensive during the cold months. Also note that schools may be canceled on snow-days, but your employer still expects you to show up at work, just get the right outfit and the right attitude.

Some of the states are more expensive to live in than others. They have high property taxes and state income taxes, which leads to higher rents and mortgage payments. These states are economic hubs with more job opportunities and better wages; as such, they are the states busting with people, for example, New York or California. Other states, like Hawaii and Alaska, are expensive because they are popular tourist destinations.

Some states are more friendly to immigrants than others. States like California, New York, New Jersey, Maryland, Georgia, Illinois, and Washington are often referred to as sanctuary states. Living in such states could be a better idea, as you will rarely feel alone. Many immigrants prefer states where they already have friends and family.

It helps to have people you are familiar with to hold your hand and guide you through the initial stages. But once you get to know your way around and are ready to move out of your host's home, you may need to think through what state you want to make your new home in.

It may appear obvious, but because it happens so often, I need to emphasize that you should not abuse the generosity and kindness of your host. Respect your host, respect their home, and most importantly, respect their spouse/partner. Some new immigrants have been known to have illicit affairs with their host's spouse, a situation that does not end well for all the parties involved. This has made many people shy away from hosting new immigrants.

If your host suddenly changes their mind about hosting you or, for whatever reason, decides they are uncomfortable with your presence in their house, then you should promptly look for alternative living arrangements. And do let them know that.

Some of these immigrants are living under so much pressure; from work, financial difficulties, or social pressures that it does not take much to blow their fuse. Consider their initial willingness enough favor and move on without unnecessary drama. In the United States, people will call the police on you if you give them trouble. And you do not want that to happen to you.

Work

"The American Dream is a dream of a land in which life should be better and richer and fuller for everyone, with opportunity for each, according to ability or achievement." James Adam (1931)

We come to this country to experience the joy of living the life of our dreams. To seize the numerous opportunities that are available in the form of a wide variety of careers and diverse business opportunities. Being the world's dominant economic power, the United States has enviable technological advancement, military prowess, and a strong currency.

Entertainment and leisure activities and facilities are countless, as are the beautiful geographical features and scenery. There is an abundance of everything just waiting to be claimed by those willing to put in the work.

The United States is a country of convenience. Everything is within reach, as is needed. Most stores and businesses operate seven days a week; day and night, with the option of home delivery. Service delivery is very efficient, and the quality of the goods is beyond reproach.

The stores are not only large but offer a wide variety of goods and services with several store associates, which ensures that you do not only shop in comfort but also that you do not waste valuable time lining up as you wait to be served. Customer service is unique and excellent, making you satisfied with your purchases. But should you not be, there is the option of returns.

For all that to be possible, the country requires a constant supply of labor to sustain the efficiency that the United States is known for. Immigrants help sustain this supply chain. We come to this country to work. To add value, even as we also enjoy the many benefits associated with working in the United States: Better and regular pay, paid time off, overtime pay (should you work beyond regular hours), health insurance, and retirement plans, amongst many others.

There is a constant demand for labor in the United States. The reason you got the migrant visa was so you could join the labor force, even if they did not tell you so. People with certain skills and talents find it easier to find work after getting their work permits.

The American job market is skills-based. Skills like tech skills, digital literacy, plumbing, hairdressing, driving, fabricating, and tile fixing, to name a few, are in constant demand. Nurses and teachers can get jobs as soon as they get their local professional licenses. Even if you do not fall within these classes, you will still find a job. That is why they call it the land of opportunities.

A new immigrant should consider getting a job priority. This is a crucial part of your adaptation process in your new home. Immigrant life in the United States is centered around work. The sooner you adopt the work culture, the better. Joining the workforce is good for you as a new immigrant because you get to connect with other people from diverse backgrounds and nationalities.

You learn more quickly about American culture, language, and manner of speaking when you constantly interact with Americans during your work. As you get challenged by seeing your colleagues' accomplishments, you grow.

Having a job will boost your self-esteem and increase your sense of self-worth. Furthermore, having a job means you do not need to depend on others to meet your daily needs. Americans hate the dependency syndrome, and attempting to depend on anyone here will quickly ruin your relationship with them.

Earning an income will not only give you independence but it will also earn you respect among the people around you. Financial freedom is very liberating and will help set the foundation for the life you hope to build in your new home.

But those are just semantics. You work to pay bills, and that is a huge deal. Life here is expensive. Everything costs money. Once you get to the United States, you automatically attract bills, which must be paid when they are due. Failure to do so has dire consequences.

As soon as you are able to, apply for your work permit—the document that allows you to work in the United States. Once you get this document, apply for a Social Security Number (SSN). Keep the card where the social security number is written very safely so it is not stolen. You can memorize the number, so you do not have to walk around with the card.

Next, apply for your state identification card (State ID). You will need the social security number and state identification whenever you apply for a job. Then, you can apply for a driver's license, even if you do not intend to buy a car yet. Many employers expect you to have it.

There are numerous job search platforms on the internet. It costs nothing to join these platforms. You just need to create an account and upload a resume, which must have your email address, phone number, and at least two referees. You can provide referees from your home country when you are just starting off, (ensure you provide their current contact information, as some employers may want to contact them).

Most of these job platforms give basic career advice, resume writing, interview skills, and suggestions of jobs you can apply for based on your resume. You can apply for as many jobs as you can find, to increase your chances of getting selected.

As much as job opportunities are advertised everywhere, getting the kind of job you want will not be that easy. Therefore, take the first job you get and do not leave it until you get another. The truth is, it may be a while before you get a job that is commensurate with your educational level (from your home country).

Your first job is likely to be an entry-level job. These jobs do not pay much, but they add up if you work many hours. You may work long hours at a particular job, or you get a second job to cover your financial obligations.

Those who come to the United States with foreign degrees and professional qualifications can take their certificates for evaluation (for example, at World Education Services) to be given US equivalence of their education and qualifications. However, they will still be expected to take professional certification examinations before they can join the local job market in their career of choice.

There are many immigrants who held professional jobs in their home countries but opt for non-professional jobs when they get to the United States. There are several reasons for this. These are the people who will work in warehouses, group homes, as caregivers, housekeepers, store associates, waiters and servers, customer care assistants, drivers, laborers, or whatever other job they can get. The pay is minimal.

However, if you have good negotiation skills, you can convince your employer to pay you according to the education and skills you have from your motherland, if you can prove you will add additional value to the job.

The job application process can take between two weeks to a couple of months. Keep this time span in mind. Your first paycheck may come three weeks after starting a new job. (That is about 5 weeks in total before your first paycheck). Most employers pay salaries on a biweekly basis. A few may pay weekly, while others pay monthly. So, plan how to go through these initial days before your first paycheck, especially as regards transportation to work.

Once you have some job, you can begin looking for your dream job. This will be a rough journey filled with many hurdles. Getting a good-fit job will not be easy. There are lots of intricacies involved that can be very discouraging. But that is no reason to give up; the end will certainly justify the means.

Work in the United States is intense. Some jobs are physically exhausting, others mentally, and many others both. Your employer/supervisor expects you to give your job full attention when you are on the clock. High expectations are set, and results must be delivered on time.

Time management is most crucial in the workplace. Everyone is expected to come to work on time and to clock in at the beginning of their work shift, and people are only supposed to engage in work-related activities for the time they are on the clock. Unnecessary use of phones while on the clock is unacceptable.

The work environment is both aggressive and impersonal. It is very individualistic, as everyone focuses on achieving their goals and career advancement. Employers encourage workers to showcase their individual strengths and autonomy, and competition amongst work colleagues is subtly encouraged.

There is a constant desire amongst employees to outperform their peers, and as such, every colleague at work is a competitor. There is hardly any social interaction between workmates.

Americans are overly ambitious; they love challenges that push them to achieve their best. Efficiency, productivity, innovation, and time management run the American economy. Therefore, do not take it personally when your work colleagues come off as conniving, abrasive, or even mean. Just be sure to work by the rules and develop some spine so people do not intimidate you unnecessarily just because you are a new immigrant. Calls for some level of emotional intelligence.

If you decide to start an entry-level job below what you envisioned, do not stress over it. Many immigrants start at the bottom and work their way up; just focus on the income. Work in this country is about economic empowerment, not social fulfillment. Some of those blue-collar jobs earn respectable amounts.

Even though no one is forced to work, the expensive life in this country is a constant reminder of how important keeping a job is. Most contract jobs stipulate that one is free to walk away from the job at any time without offering any explanation as to why, just as an employer may also terminate your services without any explanation.

This is a clause that you should not take seriously because when you apply for a new job, they will expect you to explain why you left your previous job and to provide your previous employer as your reference.

Most entry-level jobs are contract-based and pay per hour. A typical workweek is Monday to Friday, 9 a.m. to 5 p.m., which totals 40 hours of work weekly. But most people will work longer than 40 hours a week. Any hour beyond 40 is considered overtime. Most jobs pay time and a half for overtime.

Many people work longer hours than the 40 in a week to take advantage of the overtime pay. Besides, 40 hours of work in the lower cadre jobs may not earn one enough income to meet their financial obligations.

Taxes will be levied in the same manner. The overtime pay is taxed more heavily than the tax on the regular hours worked. Therefore, it makes more sense (and dollars) to have two jobs that will be taxed independently.

Some immigrants prefer to start and run their own businesses as opposed to being employed. Business opportunities are as numerous as job opportunities. Most of the businesses offer professional services. Others are in health, retail, construction, education, social services, and hospitality. Immigrants dominate services like Uber/Lyft, taxi drivers, dry cleaning and laundry businesses, and gas stations.

Many immigrants work briefly when they come to the United States just to save the required capital to start and run their own businesses. This brief stint at paid employment also allows them to learn the ropes of managing such businesses. Immigrants from non-English speaking countries find this a better route as opposed to attempting to master enough English to fit in a conventional work environment.

There are several state and federal government agencies that support start-ups and small businesses, just as there are numerous grants for small businesses, some specifically for immigrants. The process of registering a business may be long and tedious and can take several months (depending on what kind of business), but it pays off in the end.

Whether you decide to look for a job or start your own business, you need a lot of emotional intelligence to help you navigate your way around in this economy. As an outsider just coming in, there will be a lot of assumptions about you, and none of them will be positive. Learn to control your emotions and your response to people or situations.

The task will be on you to prove you deserve to be where you are, doing what you are doing. Understand that you are judged by parameters that have nothing to do with you but more to do with your kind and preformed opinions on the same. Stay focused; it shall come to pass. Many immigrants are successful entrepreneurs, and even more excel in their careers here.

The American economy runs on credit. Most purchases are made on credit, with an arrangement to pay the full price over a given period. Banks offer credit cards while numerous lending institutions offer loans, mortgages and payment plans to those who are deemed credit-worthy (based on your credit score). Your credit score will determine whether you can get these services or not as well as the interest rate charged on the facility.

Thus, as a new immigrant, you should work on building a descent credit score. Credit scores range from 300 to 850, with the lowest (300) being poor and the highest (850) being excellent, in between we have fair, good and very good. Your credit score is your tag-price. Service providers use it to gauge your ability to meet your financial obligations. Your credit score dictates several aspects of your life; for example, your chances to access loans and mortgages and the interest rates charged on the same, insurance premiums, access to rental properties, chances of getting a job amongst many other things.

New immigrants have no credit history and as such will have very low credit scores. However, this can be built with time. Apply for a credit card soon as you can but be frugal in its use. The rule of thumb is, do not use more than 30% of the available credit on that card. Secondly, pay the credit card debt when it is due, to avoid penalties.

You can build your credit score by taking affordable items on credit and making the payments when they are due. Use your credit card (not more than 30% of the value of the card) and pay the credit card debts in good time. The idea is to prove that you can pay your debts when they are due.

Again, always remember it will take some time before you can get a good credit score. Be patient. Most importantly, do not trust people who are likely to overspend with your credit card. Report to the bank immediately when the credit card gets lost or stolen. You can also lock the card from your phone so no one can use it for the time it is locked.

Education

It pays to invest in an American education. The United States of America has little regard for degrees and certificates earned in other countries. Unless you secure a job while still in your home country, once you get here, it gets complicated to rely on your foreign education to get a professional job.

Going to college locally will be your best bet. There are many advantages to this. The obvious one is that you will have a competitive advantage that is likely to get you a better job with better pay, better benefits like health insurance as well as retirement benefits. Furthermore, such jobs come with job stability, job satisfaction, and increased productivity at work.

Interpersonal relationships in professional careers are much better than in lower cadre jobs, so you are likely to have lasting friendships from both college and the workplace. Most importantly, going to college will help you achieve your American dream even faster. It is a sure guarantee that you do not get "lost" in the numbers or leave a life worse than what you had in your home country.

The education in the United States is one of the best education systems in the world. Their educational institutions have high academic standards, follow rigorous practices to maintain quality, and have excellent support systems for their students. Universities and colleges in this country are numerous and offer a wide variety of courses at various levels.

Traditionally, the academic year starts in the fall (August/September), but many colleges still offer winter and spring intakes. A few institutions offer summer intakes as well. Yet others offer admission on a rolling basis, especially for online classes.

Classes may be offered on campus, online, or hybrid (a mixture of the two). Taking classes on campus comes with the advantage of enjoying the full experience of college life. Interacting one-on-one with your professors and fellow students has many advantages beyond the most obvious one of networking. Online classes, on the other hand, have the advantage of learning in the convenience of your home, not having to travel to and from college, plus online classes usually have a rolling intake.

Most programs offer entry tests before admission. Examples of entry tests are the Test on English as a Foreign Language (TOEFL) and Graduate Record Exams (GRE). Community colleges may offer tests on proficiency in English and Mathematics before granting admission. A few programs may offer admission just with proof of high school education. Your scores on the test will determine the learning level at which you will join the college.

For those who already have a college education from their home countries and do not want to go through the education system again, there is the option of taking their academic certificates for evaluation, for example, at World Education Services (WES), to be given United States-equivalent credentials. The evaluation helps academic institutions, professional licensing bodies, and employers determine the US equivalence of foreign degrees and diplomas.

However, university education is expensive. Other than the direct college fees, there is the cost of books, stationery, and commuting to and from college. But most importantly, there is the foregone paycheck when you stop working to go to school. This is usually the biggest dilemma for many immigrants. Many resort to doing both: going to college and working part-time, a daunting task but worth the sacrifice.

Getting a scholarship or grant can be a huge relief. There are many scholarships and grants that a student can apply for. Most of them are administered through the college/campus, so they are only accessible to students who already have admission. The grants may be offered by private individuals, foundations, corporations, state governments, or federal governments. Because they are not paid back, they are incredibly competitive and have strict conditions tied to them.

The other option for raising college fees is applying for a student loan. The most popular being Federal Student Aid (FAFSA), offered by the federal government. The interest rates on FAFSA are minimal as they are subsidized by the federal government. Student loans can also be offered by the state.

If all this fails, the last option would be getting a loan from commercial lending institutions or agents. There are very many lending institutions and banks that offer student loans. Most would charge market interest rates, which are a lot higher than the FAFSA interest rates.

Still, the decision as to whether to get a college education (and acquire the huge loans associated with it) or to join the workforce and start from the bottom (and hopefully rise to the top over time) is one that an individual will have to battle with. This is a greater challenge for those already with other responsibilities, like raising a family, or for single-parent households that rely on one paycheck to meet all their financial obligations.

It all depends on what stage of life one is in and one's personal goals. However, education is an investment that will certainly yield returns on the capital invested. Most especially because education in the United States comes with an elevated level of prestige globally.

Having a degree from this country will open diverse career opportunities with chances for career progression and better remuneration.

Furthermore, when you go to college as a citizen or a permanent resident, you will pay less fees than those who come to learn in the United States as international students.

The college education process itself is very flexible, catering to varied interests and individual differences. Students go through an entire year of study before they can choose their majors for undergraduate studies. There are a wide variety of subjects and courses to choose from, ranging from the conventional courses like engineering, medicine, business or law to non-conventional majors like puppet arts, cannabis study, fermentation and everything in between.

Flexibility is also in the fact that you can decide to study full-time or part-time, online or on campus. Those who are employed can register to be part-time students and decide to do only a few units per semester and continue to do so until they have enough credits to graduate. A slow process that can take years but again, worth the while.

Most colleges and universities have active and excellent student support services that guide and counsel students in figuring out what option works best for their situation. As soon as you show interest in an institution, you are assigned a student advisor who is supposed to help you through the admissions process as well as help you decide on what courses or units to take that align with your major or career aspirations. Do take advantage of this.

From the student advisory services, you can also explore various finance options and work-study programs that may be available at your campus. You will be surprised that there may be scholarships and grants that only insiders are aware of and which can give you a much-needed lifeline.

College life is very vibrant and interesting, with all sorts of activities going on. Most campuses are located on the fun side of town, or the university makes a small township with many activities suitable for student life. The cultural diversity on the campuses is immense, as there are students from all over the world. Talk of solidarity in numbers!

College education is four years for a bachelor's degree offered by universities and two years for associate degrees offered by community colleges. A master's degree takes anywhere from eighteen months to three years or even longer. A doctoral degree is anywhere over six years.

Another unique option of post high school education in this country is the one of trade schools. These are colleges that train students in specific crafts or trades. They provide learners with hands-on training and are a less expensive, faster alternative to traditional college.

Other than these traditional learning avenues, there are also numerous short courses that are offered online that specialize in just one skill or skill set at a time. Most of them are advertised to be free but will expect you to make some minimal payment to get a certificate you can use in a job application. The courses are offered by established top universities in the country but through platforms such as Google, Coursera, ExED, and many others.

There is no shortage of knowledge in this country, and you should take advantage of this fact. Even if you cannot formally attend college, you can still learn a lot on the internet. Knowledge is power; do not be left behind in this regard.

Leisure & Pleasure

The one thing the United States is big on is glamorous life. Americans live large; everything is grandiose. Evidence of this spectacular life is seen on the highways full of flashy, expensive cars, magnificent and imposing houses, white sandy beaches, or lakes full of luxurious boats, or the huge, colorful casinos that operate day and night. Shopping malls are huge and full of expensive stores, where one item could cost the equivalent of your monthly rent!

The airports are bustling with people traveling back and forth, some for work, most for pleasure. Sports arenas are always packed with people long before kick-off time, come rain come shine. Not to mention the numerous all-inclusive resorts in various parts of the country that serve as exotic vacation destinations.

There may not be much going on during the cold months, but when the warmer weather comes, all the toys are unleashed. Summer is the time to party, go on vacation, and have all the fun your wallet (or credit card) can afford. Same as the major holidays like Thanksgiving, Christmas, Valentine's Day, the Fourth of July, and Labor Day.

Americans love every opportunity to show off their financial might. The media does not fail to remind everyone about the fun going on in various parts of the country with their dramatic commercials. The more expensive, the more alluring. Summer festivities start on the 4th of July and generally end on Labour Day!

Join the party! In your own little way. It is good for your mental health. Spoil yourself by enjoying the pleasures this country is known for, as a way of rewarding yourself for all the arduous work you do. With careful planning and the right information, you can do so without breaking the bank. For example, plan your vacations during off-peak seasons, when hotels and airlines cost much less. You can also opt for Airbnb instead of hotels. Airlines like Frontier or Spirit charge a fraction of what the other airlines charge and can be a cheaper option for domestic travel. Always compare prices before you commit to paying for any service.

The other frugal way of enjoying the numerous delights of this country is to buy secondhand items. Believe me, as a new immigrant, this is your best bet if you want to join the trendy bandwagon. A carefully chosen secondhand car will serve you just as well, since people may sell their used cars for several reasons, including because they need to upgrade (and not because the car is broken). The same goes for household furniture and kitchen appliances.

You can buy used clothes and shoes and end up with assorted high-quality goods without a dent in your wallet. There are thrift shops all over the United States. These shops sell used items ranging from clothes, shoes, jewelry, kitchen appliances, utensils, house décor, art, and even furniture. There are a lot of gems hidden in thrift shops if you have the patience to comb through the many layers of trash.

Online platforms like eBay, Marketplace (on Facebook), or Craigslist also sell authentic secondhand items. You can also benefit from the massive sales held throughout the country at particular times of the year. The biggest is Black Friday, which is held on the Friday after Thanksgiving. The other is Cyber Monday, which is the Monday after Thanksgiving. There are massive discounts on goods, especially electronics, during the Black Friday and Cyber Monday sales. Because they are exceedingly popular days to shop, there will be long lines at major stores starting early in the morning.

Several stores (and online sellers) also tend to have massive clearance sales and discounts at the end of every season. One interesting aspect of buying stuff in the United States is the return policy. You can buy and return an item (for up to 30 days) if you are not pleased with it, if you still have the original tags on it. This truly helps with purchases made online.

The tricky thing is how merchandisers are so willing to offer goods and services on credit. There are all sorts of credit arrangements that can afford you the world. Most credit cards offer cashback to the cardholder for specified purchases. Some stores offer "layover" arrangements, where a customer can arrange to pay for an item through installments and only pick up the item once it is fully paid for.

It is important to learn something new every so often. There is so much going on in this country that you may want to be part of. There are all sorts of fun activities that will provide you with a healthy way of unwinding on days when you do not go to work. Learn swimming, fishing, bowling, bicycle riding, golfing, yoga, roller skating, salsa, pottery, art, wine tasting, cooking new recipes, mixing drinks (mixology), board games, and hiking. The list is endless.

Having these social activities in your life should keep you busy constructively and help you avoid loneliness. One of the greatest downsides of life in the United States is loneliness. Social isolation and loneliness will creep on you even as you are surrounded by multitudes. It may start as homesickness, which you think will fade with time. But as time passes, you realize it is not so easy to establish meaningful human connections here, as everyone appears to be so busy with their stuff and prefers to be left alone.

Loneliness is dangerous and a threat to mental health. It increases stress levels, reduces the ability to make sound decisions, and can easily lead to anti-social behavior. It is likely to drive one to unhealthy coping behaviors or to depression. For example, many immigrants resort to taking alcohol to try to cope with the emptiness and isolation, which is risky since drinking in isolation can very soon lead to alcohol dependency. Besides, it is not easy to regulate how much alcohol one takes when they are drinking alone (in the house). Not to mention, driving under the influence of alcohol is a serious crime in this country.

As a new immigrant, you may think the loneliness problem is because of your inability to make friends. But it is not. The culture here is very individualistic; immigrants are treated with practiced politeness, but the non-verbal cues are enough to remind you to keep a safe distance. It is a special kind of rejection you cannot exactly put your finger on, but you feel it all the same. It is a phenomenon that you must experience to understand. Do not take it personally. It is replicated everywhere.

The loneliness is not only emotional but also existential. There will always be a yearning for the motherland; some regret leaving a familiar life to struggle to fit in with a life that appears very unpredictable. The regret of missing routine traditions and events back home, always wishing you could join your family and friends, especially during important family functions. You miss the familiar sights and sounds of your old life and all that was associated with it.

Loneliness is worse in the cold months of winter when you are likely to be confined indoors. Winter itself is miserable with its extremely cold weather, sometimes with snow, other times with weirdly whispering winds, and other times the sun may even be shining brightly, but still, it would be extremely cold. Winters have shorter days, so it could be dark as early as 4 p.m. That alone can mess with your head if you come from tropical countries where days and nights have equal hours throughout the year.

Try to adapt to your environment the best way you can to avoid constantly thinking about your homeland and make some human connection with the people living here. Having social skills will help improve your communication and interaction with people around you.

But you still need to take it slowly to learn the mindset of the people you interact with and adjust your communication skills to fit the situation.

Keep your expectations low and be ready for disappointments as you learn that not everyone will be interested in making a connection with you. It always pays to be open-minded and to remember not to take any rejection or reluctance to be embraced personally.

It is also important to be socially aware and keep abreast of current affairs so you can have modest communication with people and make a few acquaintances. Try to attend a few events in your neighborhood, not only with the hope of making new friends but also to experience what is going on out there and have a fun time.

If attending events in person is a challenge, then opt to watch them on television or social media. You will be amazed at how interesting it is to follow a game through live streaming; the jokes and banter by other fans will give you a stadium-like experience.

Matters of love and relationships are complicated and bittersweet! Getting married or being in a relationship will be helpful for many reasons other than the company you will have at home. But be warned that dating or having a romantic relationship is a big challenge when you are a new immigrant. The level of mistrust is unbelievable.

There will always be the assumption that you are just looking for a green card or someone to help you find a soft landing. You must give it time for the other party to build trust in you. Probably, it is because of the way immigrants are constantly vilified in the media that makes many people develop apprehension. Be prepared to encounter many stereotypes about immigrants.

Finding love in this country is a struggle. There is hardly time or opportunity to meet potential dates, as most people are remarkably busy with work-related issues. They barely have the time to go out there and meet new people. Therefore, many people resort to online dating. There are so many dating sites, a testimony that there is demand for the service. Now, to know what fish to get out of the pond!

There are absolutely no guarantees, even though many people say they met their soulmates through the process. The dating platforms differ considerably one from the other. Some charge their users; others are free. Some charge a premium with the promise that they will vet their members and weed out fraudsters. Of course, the free ones leave it to you to find your way around.

Be careful who you exchange your contact information and other personal details with. Most dating sites offer basic tips on what to do and what not to do while navigating online dating. Extra care and precaution must be taken when meeting an online date for the first time, especially when you are just starting on this journey. Have a discerning spirit and pay close attention to body language.

Do not be quick to trust people you meet online. Many times, people are not who they say they are. Some are outright criminals, others are psychos. If you suspect something is amiss, get out of the situation without unnecessary drama. Online dating is full of scammers; cut off communication with anyone who asks you for money (it does not matter what the circumstances are).

There is a belief that online dating sites are just conduits for hookups and casual sex—reconsider how you "package" yourself on the apps. Sex is very liberal and illustrative in the United States. Most people have zero chills talking about sex and sexuality just as many more are extremely adventurous and constantly pushing boundaries. Be sure of how far you want to go with anyone before getting intimate. You do not want to get into situationships that may leave you emotionally scarred.

Most immigrants prefer to date fellow immigrants. This could be less complicated, as you both would have several similarities. You still have to do your due diligence because people change a lot once they come to this country, there is no guarantee the person will have the same mindset as the people you left back home. Others may find this option self-defeatist, as it is similar to a blind man leading another.

The last option is to date someone who is still in your homeland and then bring them over to the United States to join you once you get comfortable with each other. But even this comes with no guarantees. People have been known to "import" partners from outside the United States and get dumped as soon as the partner gets themselves a better deal (read new catch). Others have supported their new spouses through school/college, only to be abandoned after the new spouse gets on their feet.

Whatever path one decides to take regarding dating and relationships, it is important to have a discerning spirit. Being naïve can be very costly, as can being vulnerable or desperate. As a new immigrant struggling to find your footing, it does not make sense to take in a lover whom you have to be fully responsible for. It will be financially draining, and sometimes ending such relationships comes with unnecessary drama that can be fatal.

On the same note, be wary of those who show you too much love too soon (love-bombing). Some of them could be having serious underlying emotional issues that could make them irrational when things do not go their way. Run if a partner you barely know takes life insurance soon after marrying you. Fatal attraction is a thing in the United States!

Ultimately, life in the United States calls for having a partner or a spouse. It is the surest cure for the loneliness here. Having a spouse is also financially beneficial, as you can share the bills and split the living costs. Moreover, people are so busy chasing their dreams that you would rarely have the time for social visits or hanging out with your family and friends. Lastly, only your spouse or partner can step in to be there for you should you be in dire need. Whichever route you decide to take towards this end, know it will be worth the trouble.

Laws & Regulations

Do not break the law! Do not get involved in anything that can lead you to the wrong side of the law. Having a criminal record will limit your chances of getting employment, housing, and government assistance on top of the jail sentence you will serve or the fines you will have to pay. You will have difficulties getting loans or mortgages and getting admission into a college. At the very worst, you will get deported.

As a priority, get the required documentation that allows you to live in the United States legally, and once you do, always ensure it is updated and renewed as required so you do not run out of status. For example, you need a work permit before you are allowed to work legally in the United States. You will also be issued a Social Security Number (SSN) that forms part of your identification documents. You will be expected to apply for a State ID and a driver's license (if you intend to drive or own a car).

Do not drive in the United States before you get a driver's license (DL), not even just around the block. Before you get your driver's license, you will be expected to take driving lessons and then take driving tests. Practice extensively for these tests so as to be adequately prepared not only for the tests but for the actual driving thereafter. The highways and expressways are intimidating, and there are numerous road signs, especially the exit signs on highways, that you need to be familiar with. You can pay for driving lessons just to be competently prepared.

The one law in this country that has messed with many new immigrants is driving under the influence of alcohol (DUI). The law is clear: no one should operate a motor vehicle after drinking a given level of alcohol. You endanger your life and that of other road users when you operate a vehicle under the influence of alcohol (and drugs). Do not argue with the traffic police when you commit a traffic offense, nor should you attempt to bribe the traffic police.

The United States is extremely strict on sexual offenses. Once you are a sex offender, it becomes extremely hard for you to get that record off. Your fate is sealed. Even worse are sexual offenses that involve children. A child sex offender is not allowed to go anywhere near where children are. With schools and daycares scattered all over, that truly limits movement.

Sexual offenses are not just physical but also emotional and mental. The offenses may be committed in person or online, and the passage of time does not prevent the prosecution of the offender. Online sexual abuse includes sending someone unwelcome nude photos or videos, sharing someone's private photos or videos and several other things that involve invading someone's privacy.

Domestic violence is a crime you will never recover from in this country. Even just being accused of it is bad enough, getting a conviction will set you back immensely. As such, do not lay your hands on your spouse, child, or anyone else, for that matter. It is considered assault; however, minor you may think it. And it does not matter what level of provocation you think you have been subjected to. Never let your emotions get the better of you. Many new immigrants have gotten into problems with the law because of this.

Use some critical thinking and quick decision making to defuse situations before they get out of hand. Even better, avoid people who are overly dramatic, people with anger issues, or people who appear not to have their act together. No good will come out of any interactions with such people. Learn to walk away from any situation that threatens to escalate, whether you think you are right or not.

If you sire a child, you will be expected to provide for that child. Even if you are not married to the mother of that kid or living together, you will still be expected to pay child support. It does not matter what the circumstances are. If you default on this, it becomes a felony, and continued failure will make it a criminal offense. You will still be expected to pay the accrued arrears, even though it will be impossible for you to get a job when you have this felony on your record.

Do not become a victim of crime. Since most Americans own and use guns, you can get shot for the flimsiest reason. It is important to be aware of your surroundings and to avoid situations that are likely to escalate. Exercise caution when meeting someone for the first time. Study the body language of the person and other non-verbal cues to assess their character (or lack of) and ability to handle pressure.

Watch out for road rage; many people have lost their lives to manic drivers. There is considerable aggression on American roads that you need to steer away from. Many drivers are fatigued and exhausted from constant commuting. Others may just be aggressive bullies who like to have their way. As many Americans are licensed to carry firearms, shooting is common during road rage. Should you feel your life is in danger, call 911 promptly, because danger here can very quickly escalate to death.

You do not have to be paranoid about the police, but unnecessary encounters with the police will not end well for you. Some immigrants have been known to call the police on fellow immigrants every time they have a disagreement. The police have more important duties to attend to than petty feuds.

Avoid being arrested. And if you are arrested, let people in your community know; hopefully, they will get you legal representation. Going to jail as an immigrant will be the second worst thing that can ever happen to you.

Avoid people who are likely to lead you down the path of crime. The United States is full of all kinds of people, and you cannot for sure know what some of these people are up to. Do not be quick to invite strangers to your house. Use your intuition.

American Culture

The United States has often been referred to as ***a melting pot.**" The cultural diversity in the country is immense. There are people from all over the world—people of different races, ethnicities, sexual orientations, religions, genders, ages, and disabilities. Each having different beliefs, values, traditions, and customs. Most immigrants learn to blend in with the local culture, knowing what to adapt and what to disregard. That said, it is imperative that you respect other people's beliefs and choices. Keep your shock and bewilderment to yourself when you realize just how different people can be.

Americans love stars. Walk like a star, dress like a star, and talk like a star, and you have everyone's attention. The opposite is also true; if you walk around looking meek and intimidated, no one will ever take you seriously. Work on your self-esteem and confidence levels. Read books or articles, listen to podcasts, or watch YouTube videos to boost your level of awareness, then go out there like you are ready to conquer the world. There are online life coaches you can hire to help.

American life is grandiose. Everything is meant to be awe-inspiring and elaborate. The houses are big, the cars huge, and their highways enormous. Everything is tailored to be large and luxurious. Burgers, pizza, fried chicken, hoagies, or whatever other foods all come in super-sizes, so it is perfectly fine to ask for a box to carry the remnants (a doggie bag) after eating in a restaurant.

Because people are always rushing to go to work or from work to whatever other places Americans are always rushing to, most of the food is eaten on the go. People hardly sit in restaurants to eat during the day. Instead, most eateries have drive-throughs where customers order and pick up their food at designated windows without getting out of the car. The food is then eaten as the person drives to their destination. However, a lot of people go out to restaurants for dinner, which is the major meal of the day.

Another common habit that gained popularity during the COVID-19 pandemic is ordering "takeouts". This has been perfected by having apps like Uber Eats or Door Dash on your phone so that, at a click, you have your meal in minutes. Most Americans do not cook, proudly so.

US English has a particular accent that can be frustrating for new immigrants, especially from non-English-speaking countries. The stretching of some letters, changing the sound of others, the intonations, and the combination of some words can all be confounding. Then, there are several slang words that a newbie may not be familiar with.

The rule of thumb is to take it slow; it will all come to you in time. Concentrate on communicating to pass information without dwelling on your accent. By no means should you be ashamed of your accent. If anything, many people would be interested in knowing where you come from so that your accent becomes an icebreaker. It is all right to ask a person speaking to repeat themselves or speak more slowly if you have a problem understanding them.

In the United States, people expect you to live independently once you become an adult. Nobody is going to be responsible for a fully grown adult, which may be very surprising for immigrants who come from countries where people believe in brotherhood and "carrying one another's burden."

American children move out of their parent's homes when they go to college at the age of 17 or 18 and learn to depend on themselves from then on. It is not strange to hear of children paying rent to their parents for living in the family home or parents taking their children to family court over some unpaid debt.

Americans love sports. The sports industry rules the airwaves. Some sports, like football and baseball, are unique to the United States. Others, like basketball, soccer, volleyball, hockey, or athletics, are played all over the world. Every city or township has a favorite sport and team they are extremely passionate about. The fanatical support for teams is so intense that even toddlers know their favorite team and their players.

Sports often make the opening line for small talk or polite conversation in social gatherings. One major social activity between fathers and their kids is teaching them the basics of their favorite game. And there is a stereotype about aggressive soccer moms!

Americans are incredibly competitive. Children learn early the need to work at being ahead of others, which is translated into the cut-throat competition that life in the United States is. *"You either eat someone at lunch or you can be lunch!"* This mindset is what builds resilience in Americans—people constantly striving to reach their goals and never losing focus until it is done.

It is important to note that a lot of this competition is also with oneself. Americans always aim to be the best version of themselves. They are not afraid to try new things or take on new challenges. They will quickly want to know about new cultures, new languages, and new cuisines. Continuing education is a thing in this country.

Individualism is a core culture in the United States. Self-reliance is encouraged. Everybody is either busy chasing their dreams or living them, and no one has the time to tag along with a clueless newbie. Your best friend in this regard is the internet. Whatever you do not know and need to know, you will find on the internet. Use Google and YouTube to get information. Your phone is your road map.

The entertainment is a huge industry in the United States. The home of Hollywood churns out new media and movie stars who earn mega-millions by the day. The influence of these celebrities is phenomenal, especially here in the United States. They dictate not only fashion trends and fads but most aspects of American life including religion and education. Do not be surprised when college professors draw examples and illustrations from the celebs.

Americans adore their celebrities and want to know every minute detail of their lives. A lot of talk shows on television are centered around the lives of these tycoons, feeding the public demand for celebrity gossip. The pop culture of these celebrities has a huge influence on the everyday life of most Americans in spite the fact that most of them live very scandalous lives.

Most movies, music and television programs are very illustrative and explicit. Sex, nudity, and violence forming the general running theme. Americans are very liberal about their sex life and freely flaunt it as such. The manner of dressing, especially in the summer, leaves nothing to the imagination. Most major cities battle violent crimes, especially gun-violence. You must always be aware of your surroundings and take safety precautions so as not to be a victim of crime.

Most Americans are deeply passionate about their political beliefs and their political party of choice. The political divide is wide and deep. There are several political parties, but the Democratic Party and the Republican Party are the most popular. The supporters of each hardly have any regard for the other. Be careful before choosing a political side, as it could lead to closed doors when you interact with people from the other end of the political divide. Immigrants are only allowed to vote once they get American citizenship, otherwise it is illegal to so before then.

Conclusion

The United States of America is a beautiful country; it has opened its doors to millions of people from all over the world; and given everyone an equal chance to work and live the life of their dreams. There are so many advantages of moving to this country as an immigrant, top on the list is the economic empowerment it can grant you, the freedom and liberty that allows you equal rights as everybody else.

Services like health, education and entertainment are way above what is found in many countries. The infrastructure is par excellence. Systems that work, the convenience with which people can get the goods and services they need and the camaraderie that immigrants enjoy in knowing almost everyone else is an immigrant all make this country incomparable.

But relocating to a new country is a major decision that comes with tons of logistical issues. Abandoning a familiar life and loved ones is not an easy decision. Furthermore, relocation is financially expensive, emotionally draining and sometimes even spiritually confusing. Homesickness is real and loneliness will erase all the joy of being in a new place. However, with the right information and proper preparation, the transition can be made seamlessly smooth. I hope the information contained in this book will help make smoother the process of navigating life in the United States of America for new immigrants!

About the Author

Betty Olela, an educator with over two decades of teaching experience, now calls Philadelphia, USA, home after spending most of her life in Kenya. As a versatile professional, she is a writer, teacher, counselor, mentor, life skills trainer, and motivational speaker. Raised by parents who were teachers, she is passionate about sharing knowledge. She also is a devoted mother to Eric and Michelle, enjoys holiday traditions with her family. She values deep connections, and maintaining strong bonds with her circle of girlfriends. Betty finds joy in travel, cooking, and unwinding through music and dance.

You can connect with me on:
- https://www.instagram.com/bettiolela
- https://www.facebook.com/olelabet